How to Make a Woman Happy

by Bret A. McClanahan

DORRANCE PUBLISHING CO
EST. 1920
PITTSBURGH, PENNSYLVANIA 15238

The contents of this work, including, but not limited to, the accuracy of events, people, and places depicted; opinions expressed; permission to use previously published materials included; and any advice given or actions advocated are solely the responsibility of the author, who assumes all liability for said work and indemnifies the publisher against any claims stemming from publication of the work.

All Rights Reserved
Copyright © 2019 by Bret A. McClanahan

No part of this book may be reproduced or transmitted, downloaded, distributed, reverse engineered, or stored in or introduced into any information storage and retrieval system, in any form or by any means, including photocopying and recording, whether electronic or mechanical, now known or hereinafter invented without permission in writing from the publisher.

Dorrance Publishing Co
585 Alpha Drive
Pittsburgh, PA 15238
Visit our website at *www.dorrancebookstore.com*

ISBN: 978-1-6442-6480-5
eISBN: 978-1-6442-6046-3

Dedicated to Minami…
YSC, and *you* know why.

Astute, as tute, adjective

having or showing an ability to accurately assess situations or people and turn this to one's advantage. Google.

Chapter One

First Impressions are Always First

On that early August Friday morning as I was curbside, dropping off Minami at the Albuquerque International Airport for her flight to Phoenix, Arizona, I could not stop thinking about what she wanted. Wow—she was really going to do this. Since she looked so radiant and oh so pretty in her all black athletic shorts and top with just the right make-up and attention to hair, nails, and such like a celebrity, I jumped out of the driver's seat and ran around to the front of my shiny all black Chevy Tahoe and gave her a big hug. "Text me when you get there and see you later tonight!" I exclaimed as the crowd looked puzzled, Minami with *no* luggage and I making such a statement.

No need to get too far ahead of myself. We need to bounce back just a wee bit less than six months ago.

It was the Saturday after Valentine's Day and I was set to meet one of my real estate buds for lunch at Twin Peaks. It was hot and sunny like a typical February Saturday in Albuquerque as I came rambling into the dead and empty parking lot. I was able to park my nasty yellow H 2 Hummer right up front near the door. Since I played high school football back in the 1980s I am quite familiar with Vince Lombardi time. If you are not ten minutes early, you are late. I am also not from New Mexico and people are so confused how I arrive so early everywhere all the time.

As I entered the front door, it was easy to notice that the place was slow with only a couple guys at the bar and virtually no one in the dining area. There she was in her petite glory wearing the signature tiny khaki shorts and red / black checkered halter top all too well known as the Peaks Girl Uniform. She was at the hostess station with her back to the door as she spun around with graceful enthusiasm and a pearl white movie star smile.

I am famous for being sarcastic so I asked, "Are you the hostess or a server?"

"Oh, I'm a server,..." she answered, still smiles away and a twinkle in her eye. I swear she had a twinkle in her eye.

"Where in the hell is the hostess? I swear they are never up here like they are supposed to be…" I slapped my open hand down on the host station counter pretending to be upset.

"I know…where is she? Never a hostess when you need 'em" Still all smiles and twinkle in her eye. Aw, sarcastic as well…Love her already.

I then suggested, "Well, if you have any open tables, I could sit in your section."

She laughed as she grabbed a couple menus and motioned me to follow her past the big moose head mounted above the fireplace and the wide expanse of open and empty tables. Mid-February is not known for a lot of sports activity on TV and the weekends this time of year are pretty slow at Twin Peaks #6 in Albuquerque. As we approached the high top table with four bar stools made with simulated logs and twigs, signature Twin Peaks, I boldly blurted out, "Tell me about the BEST part of your Valentine's this past week."

"Since I do not have a boyfriend, I did not have much of a Valentine's this year." I shit you not she was still all smiles and twinkle in her eye. "What would you like to drink? A Dirty Blonde or a Naughty Brunette?" Standard beer and questions when one dines at Twin Peaks.

"Just an ASS Tea..." I answered in a country bumpkin voice to continue being a smart ass. "...and some of that chips and queso dip... add venison chili please."

As she placed the glass on the table with a coaster she said, "Your *iced* tea." With a strong emphasis on iced. Her faux wood log Twin Peaks plastic name tag said, "Minami, Japan."

"How about if I let you take my black, stainless steel, Luxury Master Card for like say, two or three days? Go shopping and get yourself some nice things so Valentine's is not a complete bust this year?" I asked as I looked into her eyes and began to study her for Asian features. Wow, she had such an exotic look, so pretty.

As she rolled her eyes and said, "Yeah, right." I blurted in fast to save face.

"How do you say your name? Mini Me? Mena Me? "

She laughed at my efforts and answered, "My name is pronounced 'Min-Ah Mee' and my Pops is from Japan. That is why the Japan on my name tag." I gave her my business card and suggested we meet for sushi or visit about the Law of Attraction sometime. She took the card and read aloud, "Bret McClanahan, District Manager / Special Accounts New Mexico - West Texas." I explained that I represented a company that manufactures stucco and stucco-like materials all over the world, with a factory here in Albuquerque.

It was at about that point that my friend Andrew the real estate agent had arrived to join me for lunch. And as he walked up to the table, the attractive exotic looking Minami began getting other tables and customers. Our conversation was then limited, but I continued with eye contact and the use of her name. I learned that she was prelaw at University of New Mexico with serious aspirations to attend law school. She had already taken her LSATs and had a potential Harvard Law School opportunity. Minami has also noticed that I made mention of The Law of Attraction to which she told me that she read the book, *The Secret*, and she was interested in manifesting affirmations to the universe.

I was wearing a dark Lacoste, mmmm...I love that Crocodile, Levi's blue jeans, and brown Chuka Boots. I did the splits for Minami like a pro gymnast and she copied me forever in video on her smart phone. By the way, I am 220 pounds and 6' 2" with only eyebrows, clean shaved head-always. Just the other day Minami displayed the video of me doing the splits for her at Twin Peaks on the Saturday just after Valentine's Day. She told me that she was impressed with my ability since she had performed gymnastics when she was younger.

YSC...You're So Cool!

Later that day, long after I had paid my bill for lunch and departed Peaks, Minami sent me a brief text. She said in the text that now I had her number and I could text her. She asked about Law of Attraction and motivation books. I sent her via text a picture of the book by Mark Mansen, *The Subtle Art of How to Not Give a F****. I informed Minami that the book was referred to me by Mariah, a Twin Peaks girl previously, and the book was amazing. Mariah represented Albuquerque in the National Twin Peaks Bikini Competition the year before.

We started to text from time to time discussing books and a potential sushi date.

First impression is key. Make her laugh, be charming, and genuine. Be positive.

Chapter Two

Attention Cycles

I waited a week or so and then made arrangements to once again meet my real estate friend Andrew for a Saturday lunch at Twin Peaks. The regular week day bartender, Carrissa, was scheduled to fill in on Saturday. And since we knew her well from our Tuesday Happy Hour Sessions, we decided to sit in the bar area.

Actually that is partly true. I knew that Minami would be working and I wanted to pop in and sit anywhere *except* her section. Again I arrived painful early, well ahead of Andrew, and again I was able to park the nasty yellow H 2 Hummer right out front. Remind me later why I drive that beast. I was watching golf or some other off season blah sport on one of the numerous flat screen TV sets in the bar area when I noticed Minami and her petite frame in the corner of my eye. With the most obvious look, I pretended to notice her. "Oh yeah, you work on Saturday and Sunday lunch. How cool." Before she could reply, I added, "Stay right here, I have something for you in my car." I ran outside and grabbed a bubble wrap envelope handing it to her back inside.

"What is this, a book?" She asked again with all smiles and that same damn twinkle in her eye. As she opened the bubble wrap envelope, she revealed a tiny Harvard t-shirt!

"Well...we still have not made that sushi date and I stumbled across this on the internet." I explained as she hugged me super tight and screamed and jumped.

"This is so dope!" exclaimed Minami.

She went back to her section and attended tables as Andrew arrived for lunch. He mentioned something about showing homes all day and then said, "Hey, isn't that Minami? You still texting her? Has she noticed you are sitting here?"

Later that evening Minami sent a short text video wearing the Harvard t-shirt.

The very next weekend I sent a text to Minami on Sunday to ask if she was working lunch and she responded, "Of course," and suggested I come in and sit in her section. I told her that I had a million things to do but I would try. I immediately went to Sushi King and ordered $100 worth of all freaking kinds of sushi to go with soy sauce, wasabi, and chopsticks. Bang! Then off to Twin Peaks I headed in the nasty yellow H 2 Hummer. This time I parked in an open handicapped parking space since there were no open spaces up front at Twin Peaks. It was important that Minami see the big yellow beast parked out front so she knew I had arrived. It was also important for all of the other Peaks Girls to see the big yellow H 2 Hummer parked right out front in plain sight. Bret is here...with treats for Minami.

Wearing a Lacoste with khaki shorts and hiking boots, I stood alone at the host station...Ha! Go figure, no host anywhere and I caught Minami's eye way in the back near the kitchen. She lit up, smiled, and nodded her head, making the implication to walk over to her section. I nodded my head back and forth in the universal no gesture and then using all of my fingers motioned her to join me at the host station. As she was walking towards me, I lifted up two giant crazy bags of $100 worth of sushi take out with about 50 or 60 chopsticks. As she enthusiastically accepted the sushi, I told her that I had to run since I had so much to do. A big lie since I went to Suncare for a tan session right after Twin Peaks and then took the Hummer through the car wash and then home.

She gave me one of her famous hugs where she will squeeze around the ribs and bury her head in my chest just under my chin. Mmmm…her perfume is incredible.

Make yourself not too available, imply you have so much going on in your life. Push pull…nice little gestures and then bolt. Become interesting and never hang around too much.

Minami sent a text later thanking me for all that sushi and the other Peaks girls thought it was nice. I replied with YSC…meaning You're So Cool, and made up some crap that I could sure use a personal assistant. Minami asked what I needed a personal assistant to perform and I stated driving me around in my all black Chevy Tahoe and maybe Power Point presentations. Minami and I texted heavily after that. She would text and ask what would I pay a personal assistant and I would reply with a text that said,"What are you worth?" I had captured her attention.

I did *not* text her everyday.

Later in the week I sent a text to Minami and told her that we have a guy in our lab at work who never sends his wife flowers. I continued on stating that this guy says how flowers are a waste and he can not see spending money on them since flowers just croak anyway. In my text I told Minami that I send flowers to my mom on her birthday and Mother's Day. Actually true and not made up. I even told Minami that my mom sends me a thank you note, hand written, in cursive each and every time I send flowers. Minami then sent a text that said she likes getting roses.

I made arrangements with People's Flowers in Albuquerque to make a special Saturday delivery of a Luxury Rose arrangement with fifteen red roses and additional four white roses to Minami at Twin

Peaks. Bang ! You guessed it...Text on Saturday with a little video of the roses and another video later of her roses at home. During one of our text sessions, I asked Minami what her dream car would be if she could drive anything. Her answer was either a Maserati or a Range Rover.

It was now time to build trust and display that I am a man of my word.

Chapter Three

The Favor Effect, Establish Rapport, and Trust

Twin Peaks had scheduled a bikini car wash for a military charity, Folds of Honor. Outside patio tables could be reserved for a $40 fee and then cash donations accepted for car washes.

It was too difficult to pass up the opportunity. I paid the 40 bucks and instructed Andrew to gather up some guys. Andrew had recently purchased a sweet Ferrari with an ice blue-silver paint scheme from some dude in California and he was excited about bringing his new and latest toy to the car wash. It was all set for a Thursday afternoon in late April.

I asked Minami if she would like to house sit at my home for a few days while I had regional meetings in Dallas. I told her we could crash the Peaks bikini car wash and then I would give her a key to my home.

I had explained to Andrew and everyone that I would try to leave work early and go home with my all black Chevy Tahoe and I would then bring the yellow H 2 Hummer for the car wash.

In secret and as planned, I told Minami to meet me at P.F. Changs across from Twin Peaks in an area where we would not be in view of anyone. Minami would drive the Hummer to the Peaks car wash and I would spot her a $50 bill for the charity donation. After, I would give her my house key so that she could watch my home during my Dallas business trip.

I began to text Andrew and tell him that I may not have the opportunity to go to the bikini car wash because I was tied up at work. I would then text how, it was doubtful I could have the time to switch cars and go home for the Hummer.

Andrew sent me a text, "Very Funny." He continued, "Minami is here."

"Oh wow! Does she look hot in a bikini?" I sent back in text, "I did not know she would be there on a week day."

"She is here in your truck." Andrew blurted back in text.

"No-must be another black Tahoe, I am still at work." I sent in text, sitting at the bar of P.F. Changs enjoying a spicy shrimp appetizer of some sort and an ASS Tea.

"Minami is in your Hummer." Andrew responded in text and then he would not answer me after that.

I laughed out loud and explained to the P.F. Changs bartender that I was crashing the Peaks car wash with the help of a friend.

A few minutes later Minami was laughing and walking up to the bar saying she had good video of the event on her smart phone and that she had one of the managers change the $50 dollar bill into one dollar bills so she could toss at the bikini clad Peaks car washers...

I said, "Hey, I know you have class later, but how about some lunch? I know its late, at least get a glass of merlot. You would love a glass of merlot, right?" I was talking fast and not giving her any opportunity to answer, she just kept shaking her head. "Get my little girlfriend a glass of the house merlot." I said to the bartender as he poured a glass and placed it at the bar in front of Minami.

"Close your eyes and hold out your hand." I told Minami. I placed a small silver Range Rover logo key chain in her open hand.

When she opened her eyes with surprise, she exclaimed ,"Do you own a Range Rover?"

"Not yet." I replied. "I have been looking for some time and it was strange how you told me that a Range Rover is one of your dream cars. Hold onto this key chain and use some of that Law of Attraction affirmations and see what happens."

"Yeah, okay I will." Minami boasted. "This is cool."

That same night Minami displayed a picture on Instagram of her hand holding the Range Rover key chain with the caption, "Momma's New Baby."

I told her that I forgot a copy of my house key, but if she came over later some evening I would get her a key so she could house sit while I was in Dallas. She visited my home the very next night and she arrived in tiny denim shorts and a crop top athletic top...wow does she ever have some mighty sexy abs to compliment her smile and twinkle eyes. Oh...and great set of legs too.

Now, I possess a BA in fine arts from The Colorado College in Colorado Springs and I am a bit different. My home is in a nice midcentury modern style and super OCD clean, despite how I am a man living alone with no maid or cleaning service. My back yard is a zen garden with a Buddha statue, red Japanese bridge, a gong, green grass, trees, gravel, pavers, stepping stones, a small pond with fountain, a bamboo wall back drop...One would never believe that I live on the West Mesa in Albuquerque. My zen garden looks like Osaka, Japan. My guest bed room has a bamboo accent wall, Asian theme furniture like a red lacquered glass door cabinet with another Buddha statute. I have a Chinese Wok on my stove and yes...chopsticks in my silverware drawer. I have never visited Asia and only have left the U.S.A. to visit Mexico... Obviously Minami was super impressed with my pad. She said that she really liked the dry stack ledge stone on the high wall between the kitchen and living room. I was always a fan of MTV Cribs and thus, I have a giant double door stainless steel fridge. I keep that monster fridge stocked with all kinds of juice, drinks, Dasani bottled water, Perrier, S.Peligrino, Jose Cuervo Tequila, margarita stuff, vodka…and the like. An open cabinet displays nice restaurant quality dishes, bar ware, Champagne flutes, wine glasses, cocktail shakers. I even showed Minami all the crisp white extra clean towels and linen for all the beds in my home. I also have a spare purple plastic toothbrush in the original new package from Walgreens in the event of an emergency over night guest. I had a subscription of Maxim magazine way back around 1998 and it said to keep a new toothbrush for emergency guests. Clean T shirts for an unexpected house guest to sleep in. Most important, change the sheets and pillow cases on your bed each and every freaking week. Always be ready to impress a woman…and make her happy.

As Minami and I stood in the giant master bedroom at the foot of my bed, also in a mid-century modern motif, I said to her, "Only one major rule when you stay at Bret's home. No sex with anyone else in Bret's bed or on the dining room table."

"Well, since I don't have a boyfriend right now, that should not be a problem." Minami snapped back while she fluttered eye lashes and a smile.

"You do not need a boyfriend to have sex, silly." I always try to have a quick come back. "You may have hot lesbian sex in my bed but stay off the dining room table. Oh, and try to get video. Other than that, off limits having sex with anyone else in my bed."

She laughed and kind of appeared to be in shock with my candor. "I can't wait to stay here at your home, Bret. I am going to read all of your books." Again and again Minami would tell me how she was a self-proclaimed "Nerd" and was an "old Lady" in high school-chubby, studious, and wearing glasses. She was the president of her DECA Club, she had a stake in a water machine franchise after graduation, and she played a little with penny stocks online. Introverts can be so damn sexy.

Yeah, Minami liked my cool home right off the bat. She was set to watch the place while I was in Dallas. I encouraged her to pop over often anytime.

"With the Hummer and the Tahoe hogging up all of the available space in my garage, if I get a Range Rover, do You have covered parking at your apartment complex?"

"Duh, Hell yeah. We have garages. If you want me to watch your Range Rover, I will get a garage to park it." Minami said with an extra twinkle in her eye.

"We may need to take a test drive soon." I added. "I have been looking around the area and there are a few Range Rovers that I like. Late model and low miles."

It was a Thursday morning and my year to date sales were in the tank. Way off and way down compared to previous year. All of my accounts were doing quite well with the exception of one single account. When that particular account was down, I was down. My sales report looked awful.

I had been corresponding over the magic of the internet and narrowed my Range Rover search to a single car lot in Albuquerque. Black metallic five year old with low miles Range Rover Sport. I sent an email to the sales manager and told him I would come by before lunch. I contacted Paul, my insurance agent, to inform him of my pending purchase. Since I was at work, I was driving around in the all black Chevy Tahoe. Mmm…love that car with old school chrome rims. Nice vehicle. I parked right smack in the front of the car lot and the white haired, golf tanned, old movie star sportscaster looking sales manager met me and inquired, "Are you Bret? Let me get the keys and we can take the Range Rover you are interested in out for a spin."

I walked up to him and said, "If it's okay with you, I am on my lunch and pressed for time. Let's just start the paperwork. I have four credit union accounts with savings at Wells Fargo and Bank of America with an 822 credit score. One of my credit union accounts was started by my mom in 1966 when I was one year old and that particular account has been uninterrupted all these 50 or more years." Dennis, the golf tanned sales manager, said later that it was on record as his most fastest sale ever…just under an hour.

As I zipped off the lot in my new / pre-owned, second hand, but oh so sweet and special Range Rover, I said that I would be back shortly for my all black Chevy Tahoe. The Range Rover was on fumes and nearly out of gas. Why car dealers do that shit is beyond me. I just purchased a freaking car, put some damn gas in the beast. As I was driving home, it suddenly occurred to me that Andrew, my real estate contact, was out of town. Evan, Andrew's boss, who I have known since moving to Albuquerque in 1998, twenty years ago, was also out of town. Damn, once I get the Range Rover home, how will I get back to my all black Chevy Tahoe still parked at the dealer? Quick thinking while I crossed over the Rio Grande on the Montano Bridge, I sent a text to Orlando, Sales Manager with L&P Supply, one of my top accounts. I explained that I was stranded at my home. He said he would be there in about twenty minutes. Orlando sent a text later that he was "tide" up and could not help me today. Orlando came to the U.S.A. from Mexico as a kid, became a citizen and yadda, yadda, here he is. English is his second language so yes…he sent in a text that he was "tide" up. Oh well, he tries and he gets the point across. I could not help but picture an orange jug of Tide laundry detergent as I looked at the text from Orlando and I knew I needed to get back to my all black Chevy Tahoe and subsequently return to a productive day at work.

Just so everyone understands, I wake each day Monday to Friday between 4:30 A.M. and 5 A.M. I set my alarm for 5 A.M., however pretty much wake, no matter what on my own between 4:30 and 5 even on Saturday and Sunday when I am off. We take, as a company, a two week vacation each year right around Christmas-from about December 16 to January 3, and it is amazing. Anyway, my body still gets my ass out of bed between 4:30 A.M. and 5 A.M., even if I party like a rock star and stay up late. After rising so early, I get on the computer and address email as well as log calls on our Sugar CRM. I have a light breakfast, shower, shave my face and entire head like Lex Luthor, head out around 6:30 A.M. and visit my million dollar accounts. From there, now around 8 A.M., I visit other accounts, job sites, travel, visit the Albuquerque Plant where I have an office, meet with Wes, the plant manager, and have operations meetings or any number of activities. My day often centers around a power lunch meeting with clients at Papadeaux's, Billy's Long Bar, Horse and Angel Tavern, or Twin Peaks. Yeah, power lunch almost each and every day. I typically arrive home around 6 P.M. and then often work on the computer until 9 P.M.. Since our corporate offices are in Anaheim, I get email correspondence into the evening due to them being one hour behind New Mexico. I like to reply right away, or I just wait until 4:30 A.M. to be a pain, in hopes their smart phone is next to their head while the unfortunate fool is sleeping.

    I wanted to go to Twin Peaks on Saturday and just walk up to Minami and hand her the key fob to the Range Rover. Screw the Saturday Twin Peaks surprise, I needed a ride, I was building rapport with her, and I do not use Uber. I sent her a text and explained that I was stranded at my home. She sent a text saying, "NO problem, be right there." Whoa, I was impressed but not surprised.

    Minami nearly shit a brick with a sharp corner when she arrived and the Range Rover was in my driveway. "SHUT UP! Can I drive that to class later?"

    "It's out of gas and I still need to get the insurance cards, but yeah, swing by later." I said as I slid into the passenger seat of her Ford Fusion energi.

She drove me back to the car dealer and when I walked up to my all black Chevy Tahoe, Dennis, the white haired golf tan sales manager, ran up to me, "Hey, did you drive that Range Rover back? We like to get pictures of everyone for our web site."

I almost laughed and did my best not to be a smart ass, "No, I had a friend drop me off so I could get my all black Chevy Tahoe removed from your lot."

"Oh, well can you come back in a day or two or maybe when your license plates are ready, so we can get a picture?"

From there I went to see Paul, my insurance agent. I asked if I could add Minami on my policy because she may be driving the Range Rover often. After Paul said, "Sure." He explained that they would need some of Minami's information. Oh crap…this is when and how I found out Minami was only 20 years old and would not be 21 until later in July. Wow, major faux pas. Minami was very flattered by the insurance cards with both my name and her name. Often it is the subtle details.

When I ordered her that glass of wine at P.F. Changs, the afternoon when we crashed the Peaks car wash, I honestly thought she was between 24 and 26 due to the way she carried herself. Ooops. Sorry, P.F. Changs.

Minami returned to my home via Uber and waltzed right in through the front door since she now had a key to my home and I had encourage her to pop in anytime. We went for a short ride around the block with her driving the Range Rover, now with a full tank of gas and the ever important and required by law insurance cards. Minami gave me a sweet kiss on the cheek and off to her class at UNM.

To make a long story short, that was pretty much the *last* time I drove the Range Rover, the very day of purchase, from the dealer to my home and then to get a tank of gas. We always referred to the vehicle as "her" Range Rover and never "my" Range Rover or even "the" Range Rover.

By all means, please keep reading. The story gets better. Oh yeah, I made a woman happy up to this point and the ability to *top* a free Range Rover would be tough.

Chapter Four

The Dallas Business Trip, Additional Rapport, and Super Trust Building

Minami insisted that I allow her to drive me to and from the Albuquerque International Airport in "her" Range Rover for the Dallas business trip. I explained to her that I had an expense account for such things and that I was accustomed to driving my self to the airport in the all black Chevy Tahoe. And I subsequently parked in the city operated covered lot right next to the terminal.

During our Dallas meetings I confided in my boss, Joe, the central region sales director. Joe was cool as hell. A Texan from San Antonio, he was super professional with a nice crease down the front of his slacks, dress shirts, awesome cologne. Very Smooth and cool. However, he was the only Texan I knew who never ever wore cowboy boots. Our corporation merged with the business that Joe founded founder years ago. Very slick man! Joe always had dress shoes or loafers, polished like a senator in Washington. I am always in cowboy boots and wear exclusively Ralph Lauren pin stripe dress shirts. I have a lot of nice dress pants but mostly for work I wear black Dickies pants…I cut off the Dickies tag on the back with an

Xacto Knife. Often, like on special Twin Peaks Fight Nights or on the popular Tuesday happy hour, I wear a nice black blazer with a crisp white pocket square. I have a cologne rotation, Abercrombie and Fitch Woods, Polo Red, Dolce and Gabbana Blue, CK One, Stetson. I only wear dark colored Lacoste polo shirts for casual attire because I love that little crocodile and ever since I read the Official Preppy Handbook way back during the Reagan administration when I was in high school.

We are getting side tracked, but anyway, I told Joe about Minami and how she was watching my home during the Dallas meetings. I displayed pics of her on my smart phone as well as "her" Range Rover. I explained to Joe that it was all my reckless strategy to anchor my head into boosting the sales in New Mexico. Joe took one look at the half Japanese, half Italian, petite, exotic Minami and said, "Jayzuhs, I am jealous, buddy." Another very cool aspect of Joe is how he says "Jayzuhs" all the freaking time.

Often my stories are difficult to follow and seldom make sense. While I was in Dallas, Andrew, the real estate agent, was also in Dallas to deliver a classic Toyota MR2 he owns, for special repairs. Andrew is a race car dude, so he has a big bad white Toyota Tundra and of course, a sleek flatbed trailer, the rig he used to bring back his Ferrari from California a few months prior. Anyway, our business meetings ended on Thursday, allowing the group free to leave on Friday morning. Since my flight was not until 4 P.M., I sent Andrew a text to swing by the hotel and pick me up. The drive from Dallas to Albuquerque would get us home around 6 P.M.

Long ass drive but fun just shooting the shit and visiting. We stopped in Amarillo for lunch at Cheddar's because Andrew was pulling that big crazy trailor and Cheddar's was easy off and easy back on Interstate 40, which was also under heavy, pain in the ass construction smack down the center of Amarillo. Sitting at lunch I began sharing some of Minami's text messages about how she "loved" staying at my home and how she wants to just move in and stay there. Minami sent a few selfie pics with that famous movie star killer smile and those eyes. Mmmm, she had one laying on the lawn near the pond in my Zen garden…way too sexy.

"You would not seriously allow her to move in, would you?" Andrew asked.

"I think that may be too late." Was my reply.

If you are paying attention, you know that my all black Chevy Tahoe is parked at the Albuquerque International Airport. Andrew offered to swing by so I could retrieve my vehicle. "Are you crazy?" I yelled,"Hell No. I plan to ask Minami to take me there in 'her' Range Rover on Saturday afternoon once she is done with her shift at Twin Peaks."

As soon as I entered through the front door of my home, the Channel perfume hit me so heavy and thick that I could have cut it with a knife. My bed had the Minami and perfume aroma as if the little shit dumped an entire bottle on my pillow. I was flattered. My home was super clean. I had left a KIVA Juice plastic gift card and $60 cash in twenty dollar bills with a short hand written note about, enjoy your stay, thanks a million, use the cash for gas or incidentals, yadda, yadda, yadda, I will text you upon my return. Oh yeah, and I pointed out the Sam's Choice Chicken Strip Doggie Treats to feed Roxy, the neighbor's dog, through the slats in the fence. I watched Roxy as a puppy once when my neighbors were on vacation. Roxy and I bonded. Minami, following my instructions, would "treat" Roxy during my Dallas trip.

I asked Minami the next day, Saturday, via text message if she could take me to the Albuquerque International Airport so I could retrieve my all black Chevy Tahoe. Obviously Minami said yes and let me know that she would be finished with work around 4 P.M. I remained as patient as possible, and I had transportation by means of my nasty yellow

H 2 Hummer anyway. I had actually made a run to Walmart for groceries and even a session at Suncare. I went to Massage Envy where I have had a membership since pinching my sciatic nerve and learning of the benefits of massage. I transferred about six of my free one hour sessions that I had accumulated to Minami for her use. I would tell Minami that I had transferred a single one hour free session, and she would find out that it was actually six free one hour sessions when she made an appointment for her initial visit. I told her to request Sabrina, my therapist, who I always insist take care of my needs. Over the years I have given way over the top cash tips, KIVA Juice gift cards, and the like for Christmas and birthdays to Sabrina. Minami would be impressed for sure when Sabrina would most certainly blab about the years of being the massage therapist of choice for Bret.

Despite her shift at Twin Peaks ending at 4 P.M. that Saturday, Minami did not arrive at my home in "her" Range Rover until after 6 P.M. Take my word for it, she looked so *hot*. Always such perfect make up and nails. She had on a white hoodie sweatshirt and that famous movie star smile. Yeah, not to sound corny, but the ever present twinkle in her eye as well. Makes for an easy eye contact scenario. She went on and on about all my books, *The Art Of War*, *How to Win Friends and Influence People*, *How to Be a Badass*, *How to Be CEO*, and so on. Minami mentioned how she slept in my bed and loved my home and the Zen garden. I reminded her that she was welcome- more than welcome, to visit anytime, even when I was not home. I said, "You have a key, pop in anytime."

"Oh, I will," Minami responded, "And I will do my homework at your place and just hang out. You really should write a book on how to make a woman happy." Minami would tell me that and text that over and over again.

We talked about how we still had not met for a sushi date or at least dinner at JinJa. Minami said that we should make plans soon. I asked her to drop me right in the front of the terminal so I could run into the parking structure and get my all black Chevy Tahoe. As I watched Minami drive down the ramp from the terminal in "her" Range Rover, I knew that in a way I blew it and had lost my nerve. It was early on Saturday night in May and I had made significant progress in the pursuit of how to make this woman happy. I admit it. She looked so amazing in "her" Range Rover driving me to the airport. Wow, where was this all going?

I would have People's Flowers send yet another luxury rose arrangement to Peaks for Minami on a Saturday delivery as a thanks for watching my home while I was away on business in Dallas. Andrew and some of his friends, including Dan (Daniele) a tall Twin Peaks bartender, were in a volleyball league that met at 6 P.M. every Tuesday. We would meet for late afternoon happy hour and sit at the bar area so Carrissa could serve us. During one particular happy hour, I received a text from Minami asking if I were at home and how she wanted to swing by in "her" Range Rover and take me out for sushi. Oh Snap! How freaking cool is that? It was very close to 6 P.M. anyway and the crowd was paying tabs and getting ready to head over to their volleyball league.

I drove home right after a quick Suncare tan session. I took a shower, changed into my favorite grey Lacoste and kahaki shorts, and waited. And I waited...and waited. I went outside in the Zen garden and began to water the lawn. When I noticed something out of the corner of my eye through the glass patio door I turned to reveal Minami standing in the living room. Yes, obviously she had that same killer movie star smile and twinkle in her sexy eyes. Always such a source of positive. We did not go out that Tuesday night. Instead we visited about Zen, Buddha, the Law of Attraction, and how everything happens for a reason. Minami explained that she was Buddhist since her pops was from Japan. She asked why I had the immaculate Zen garden with Buddha statue and the Asian room. I told her that I enjoyed living in the now present and I followed Buddha but with no formal introduction. While I appreciated the Spanish, Mexican, and Native Architecture and culture of New Mexico, I wanted a different and original home. My dad was in the Vietnam war as well as his younger brother. I guess at an early age I had Asian exposure with the dolls and curious brought back that my grandparents had in their home from my dad and uncle. Minami asked why I had chopsticks in my kitchen and I concluded that I like the best "props" like in the movies and when I eat Asian food, I like to use chopsticks. I pointed out the frozen Asian entrees in my giant M TV Cribs monster stainless steel fridge with freezer drawer. We had a few hours of bonding at my home that Tuesday evening. She asked questions and I answered honest and truthful without the wit and sarcasm from before. Most important, I listened to Minami. Tonight was her time. So yeah, I listened.

Minami had made a comment in passing that her lease was about to expire at the end of May and she would leave her apartment and possibly move in with her parents way over on the heights. I reminded her that she had keys to my home and she was welcome, more than welcome to visit anytime,…do homework, anything, unannounced, even if I were not home. Then in a moment of temporary insanity, I told Minami, "Maybe for your senior year it would be a good idea to live with your parents so You can better concentrate on your studies and gear up for law school." WTF was I thinking? Wow,…the alarms were going off in my head,…like those old Star Trek episodes with Captain Kirk and Spock,….*Red Alert,…Red Alert,…eeek,….eeek,….eeek,….*

Minami sent me a very sexy pic over text of her in some lingere on her giant California king bed with spa hotel style padded custom luxury headboard. She mentioned her dark tan and how I should try

Sun in a Million just once and take a break from Suncare. Damn toasty and sexy dark tan…Yeah, oh yeah…Minami knows how to push my buttons and grasp my attention for sure.

When Dennis, the white haired golf tanned sales manager, called to inform me that the State of New Mexico MVD (Motor Vehicle Division) had shipped the license plates for "her" Range Rover, he stated that he would fasten the plate on the rear of the vehicle and he would snap a pic so the dealership could then post on their website. I alerted Minami and with great zest she gathered me at my home and off we went for license plate install and celebrity photo op. Yeah,…of course she looked *hot* in tiny athletic shorts and crop top show off her cut abs. She goes to the gym daily and her body is obvious to the numerous gym sessions.

I have visited the website for A Star Motors on Menaul in Albuquerque oodles of times and to this day, I have yet to see the pic of Minami standing in front of "her" Range Rover holding a classic New Mexico yellow license plate with the A Star Motors office in the background. Oh well…I will keep looking.

As we drove away from the car dealer Minami made a joke about how some of the girls at Peaks asked her if Bret was her Sugar Daddy.

I cut Minami off in mid sentence and remaining in George Clooney calm, cool, and collected voice stated, "Listen…let's get one thing clear. I am *not* your Sugar Daddy or your boyfriend."

That was one of the few times I ever noticed Minami with out her killer movie star smile and famous twinkle in her eye as she quietly said, "I know."

To attempt to save face, I added that the car insurance cards list her as "household member." Ugh, how could I be such a Nazi bastard? We were having so much fun today. Not sure what the hell came over me. I was doing such an incredible job in my quest to make a woman happy.

I ordered one of the new all black Chile Capital of the World New Mexico license plates in a vanity issue with ASTUTE stamped on the metal to replace the classic yellow license plate sent to the car dealer. It was explained to Minami that although she was already a standout, the ASTUTE plate on the rear of "her" Range Rover would be a classy touch. The vanity plate with ASTUTE arrived promptly in the mail and Minami drove over to my place so that we could install the plate. I had also ordered a sweet custom chrome plated special Range Rover license plate frame. Minami had previously made plans with her mom so she did not stay long. Her mom is deaf and they communicate with sign language- another special cool Minami quality. She is close to her family. Soon it would be time for Minami to leave her apartment as the lease expired.

It was Friday at Twin Peaks and I was having lunch in the bar area with Evan and Andrew while Carrissa was our server. Carrissa had been voted to represent Albuquerque in the National Twin Peaks Bikini Contest. She was cool and was on Andrew's golf team last summer in the Home Builder's Association Golf Benefit that my company acts as a major sponsor each year. I recall Bobby from ProBuild asking,"A Twin Peaks girl on the golf team? Can she even play?"

"Does not matter," I would answer, "She does not have clubs."

Anyway,...that is a completely different story. Minami called me rather than texted and since Peaks was a crazy busy mad house that particular Friday lunch I had to excuse myself from the table and sit near the host station just so I could hear my phone. Minami explained that the movers she hired loaded her POD storage unit like fools and before she had the POD hauled from her apartment to the storage facility, would I have time tonight to look at the unit to determine if it was travel worthy. Of course I would never turn down an opportunity to meet under any circumstances or opportunity.

"Swing by in 'your' Range Rover tonight and take me to your apartment." I told Minami.

I waited...and I waited...and waited. Around 7:30 P.M. I sent her a texr to confirm that tonight, *this* Friday was when she wanted me to take a peek at her POD to ensure her belongings were secure and would make the journey from apartment to POD storage facility.

"I am just leaving Nini's nails." Minami sent in a text message. "I got a mani-pedi."

WTF? She is getting a mani-pedi? I went outside in the Friday May evening and started to water the lawn of my Zen garden. As before, I noticed movement in my living room via the glass patio door. Holy crap did Minami ever look sexy. Her athletic petite Japanese-Italian frame was in a form fitting dark grey evening dress. Damn Minami has such sweet legs. Yeah, before I go on, yes, yes, killer movie star smile and twinkle in her eye. We took a peek inside the POD but it was so dark and clearly from what I could tell, everything was adequately strapped down for the truck to deliver her POD to the storage facility. We returned to my place and made egg rolls and ate them with chop sticks. Her feet were too cute to resist so I offered to provide her with a foot massage and she answered silently with an affirmative nod of her head. As we sat on my green L shaped sofa sectional in my mid century modern living room with Hip Hop videos on BET droning on my TV, I asked, "You have a key to my place. Why don't you just stay with me for a while?" It was like I was possessed by the Devil. "Have that company drop off that POD in my drive way and you could just move in. I have the room."

"Really?" Minami asked. "I'm not sure, I've already started to stay with my parents and I already paid for the POD storage."

"Well, just something to think about." I said looking at the TV and avoiding eye contact with Minami. "I bought the house in 2001, it's nearly paid for, and the utilities are cheap. I do not expect anything from you. Keep the home clean and maybe pitch in for groceries and food."

"Yeah, I will think about it, but for now it looks like I will just stay with my parents again." Minami said, now also looking at the TV and avoiding eye contact with me.

"It still may be best to live with Mom and Dad that senior year of UNM so you can focus on Law School." I added.

YSC…*You're So Cool!

The following Wednesday, Minami sent a text asking if I could meet her at the POD storage so she could rearrange her things and grab a few items. The facility was right down the street from my office at the Albuquerque plant so of course I told her to name a time and I would meet her. It was late afternoon and hot as Sub Sahara Africa. Her giant California king bed was placed perpendicular across the POD so that anyone was prevented access to the rest of the items. Minami contemplated calling the same doofus movers she had hired in the first place who screwed up the placement of her items in the POD.

"Oh hell no!" I emphatically said. "Let me call Cisco, he is our maintenance engineer and operations coordinator at the plant right up the street. He is a big stocky guy like me and the two of us can rearrange this POD in an effective manner."

About the time Cisco arrived, the POD storage manager offered to provide Minami a new and empty POD so that Cisco and I could re-load her things. We must be clear, only Minami would have an offer from the POD storage facility like that. You or I would never get a new empty POD to remove and load our stuff. Other than breaking a giant mirror negligently stacked behind the mattress, we broke nothing and had no issues. It was so freakishly hot. I worked in a white T shirt after removing my Ralph Lauren pinstripe dress shirt. Minami wanted *all* of her shoes and a bunch of boxes so we over loaded "her" Range Rover and the all black Chevy Tahoe. I cannot express the term "over loaded" enough. I had *no* visibility in the Tahoe using my rear view mirror. Yes, it was that many boxes.

Cisco asked, "You taking all that stuff to your place?"

"No." I sternly answered, "Minami is moving back in with her parents."

"Yeah sure." Cisco rolled his eyes. Cisco had been a DJ back in the day with KISS 97 FM Albuquerque's best Hip Hop and R & B. He has a successful DJ business on the side doing weddings and graduations each weekend. Cisco was hip to the ways of the world.

I helped Minami drop off her boxes fast and furious with no parents around. I retreated off to a Suncare session and then home. I have unlimited tan sessions and I go often. Moving Minami's stuff would not slow down my tan momentum.

Chapter Five

The Big Pay Off—We Built Trust and Rapport

I empowered Minami with small and big favors. I displayed my interest with gifts / tokens big and small. I made her laugh and built trust. I was as honest as possible and did my best to make her feel special. No pressure ever and a near almost reverse psychology so that *she* could come to her own conclusions.

How to make a woman happy. I would like to believe I was doing a paramount job.

The very next day, Thursday the 7th of June, Minami started to send text messages about how to dispute Wells Fargo credit card transactions because she did not want to pay the clowns who screwed up the loading of her POD and the subsequent shattered mirror precariously stacked behind the mattress. I had a sour burning feeling in my gut like an acid would burn a whole through my belly.

I knew what was coming.

My phone rang and it was Minami. Texting was over. She was serious and obviously wanted to talk.

"Hello Minami" I acknowledged her from the caller ID.

"Hey, I have a question…" She started and paused.

"Yes?" I said now feeling like I just may crap my pants. I started to sweat and my mouth went dry as if I were sucking on cotton balls. I had been pacing around but now sat on my L shaped sofa sectional in the mid century modern living room with dry stack ledge stone all the way up to the vaulted ceiling.

Here it comes...are you ready for this?

"Well, ...I was wondering how serious you are about me moving in with you? Could I stay in that Asian room? How much would you charge me for rent?" Minami was confident and assertive.

"No rent...come on over, bring your things when you are ready." I said with my voice cracking as if I had just reached puberty.

"Great!" Minami yelled, "You're the best, Bret. I already dropped off a few things while you were at work today and I have my car loaded now...be right there."

Oh shit. I ran into the guest room with Asian motif and there were boxes of Minami's things. I started to clear out the stuff from the closet. Every so often momentarily counting the days with my fingers. Met her on February 17 and this is June 7...and she is moving in...Wow...a hot Twin Peaks woman is moving in with Bret.

When Minami arrived in her Ford Fusion energy, she had it loaded down heavy with boxes. I had moved the all black Chevy Tahoe so that she could move in through the garage.

"Yeah, I got into it with my little sister. She is still in high school and she has this attitude telling me I shouldn't move back home." Minami was excited as she spoke. "WTF, she is taking up three rooms at my parents house, Bret. Three rooms. So I told her, 'Fuck this, I'm staying with Bret' and so I started to bring my stuff over."

The next several trips were made with "her" Range Rover. Damn she has so much clothes and shoes and stuff,...like one of those Kardashian sisters. Each trip Minami would make comments like, "I'm going to cook yummy food for you, Bret. I will keep your house so clean, Bret. I will do your laundry, Bret."

I sent via text a pic of the room with all of the very recognizable Minami possessions boxes to Cisco and Cisco sent the ever popular text, "LOL " with an "I told YOU, Bro."

I sent a text back to Cisco, "I should have seen this coming a mile away. I guess I was in denial. Allow a HOT twenty year old drive a Range Rover, 'her' Range Rover and give her keys to my James Bond – Dean Martin luxury mid century cool pad with dry stack ledge stone…"

Cisco sent another text, "LOL- I saw this from five miles away. Good luck."

Out of shear panic, nervousness, and the fact that I usually run a load of laundry on Thursday night- white towels, T shirts, and Ralph Lauren white boxer briefs , I started that load of laundry and proceeded to pace around my home.

Minami stopped returning with her boxes. I started to watch old Seinfeld reruns on TV and at mid night I sent Minami a text message, "Is everything okay?"

After a five to ten minute pause, Minami answered via text, "Yes, I'm just talking to my pops."

I went to work on Friday morning hyper as all hell and bouncing off the walls. I did not sleep much the previous night. I made brief visits to my million dollar accounts and made my way to the Albuquerque plant. Often on Friday I buy breakfast burritos for the crew and have an operations meeting with Wes, the manager. Wes called in the order for breakfast burritos and he and I drove to Blake's Lot-A Burgers in his truck. I briefed Wes on my recent caper. He was about five years younger than me, but also divorced with adult kids. He just shook his head, "How old are your kids?"

I answered with, "My son is 25 and my daughter turns 29 this month in June. My daughter is in her final year of pharmacy school. Don't think my kids will care about Minami. My son now lives in Arizona"

Back at the Plant, Cisco asked me if Minami was all moved in and I explained how she stopped bringing boxes and then the text about visiting with her dad. Oh well, that was a close one.

Cisco added, "She will be there when you get home today."

To that I replied with, "Naw, she works at 4 P.M. to close at Peaks tonight."

I attempted to be as productive as possible until I had an overwhelming urge to just go home and see if Minami was there.

My home is second from the corner on my street. As I rounded the corner and immediately noticed "her" Range Rover backed into the driveway, I had a huge sigh of relief.

I entered through the garage and all of her moving boxes were broken down and stacked in the hall. I peeked into the spare Asian room and she had essentially turned the entire room into her own walk in closet. She was seated on her knees in a black silk camisole doing her make up and eyes in a mirror. She also had a load of laundry going and it was evident in the bathroom from the wet towels and steam that she had just had a shower. Wow, Minami was moved in. As she placed her laundry which consisted of the Peaks uniform, tiny khaki shorts and red with black checkered halter, including her black Peaks logo money pouch, in the dryer she maneuvered into the kitchen where she placed a microwave cup of frozen Asian Chicken Chow Mein meal. She then rustled off to the bathroom to work on her hair. I was in tow following her.

"Look, let's just say you are my house guest." I said, "I hate the term roommates and you are more like my house guest anyway."

"Suites me," Minami said as she darted back to the kitchen with the sound of the microwave alerting us that her noodles were cooked. She grabbed a set of chop sticks from the drawer, a paper towel and

Siracha sauce, and sat at the table. She started to devour her lunch with the chopsticks, stopping to blow on each bite to cool the chow mein. When the dryer went off, she was up and running. It was like a well choreographed dance production. Suddenly at 3:20 P.M. she was in her full Peaks uniform, telling me, "Bye, Bret." And then she was off and away in "her" Range Rover. And, most important, my home was clean and organized and now super quiet without her. I went back to work and visited the job sites for Legacy Apartments and the Broadstone Apartments at Northpointe. I even had time to see Bobby and Kenny, two of my strong distributors, before they closed and went home for the weekend.

Minami went to the gym every day and thus, she wore gym wear often. All in black and seductive. She looked good. Minami mentioned that she liked the healthy food in my fridge. We did start to add almond yogurt, since she was lactose intolerant, right next to her almond milk used in her protein shakes. I stepped up the quantities of chopped frozen spinach and imitation crab legs, which was Alaskan Whitefish. Since I have OCD really bad, everything was nice and neat organized in clear containers with red lids from Walmart. I bought Minami a digital scale and a plastic measure cup to mix her protein shakes when she said she would start a body sculpting competition training program.

"You are like the only person with OCD as bad as me." Minami told me after I asked her about front facing all the water and juice bottles in the monster stainless steel M TV Cribs fridge. She cleaned the goop on all the sauce bottles, ketchup, mustard, Siracha. Minami even cleaned the fabric softener residue on the inside of the washing machine. I was impressed but not surprised.

YSC…You're So Cool!

I added a medicine cabinet in the spare bathroom for Minami with three floating shelves. I asked if I could order some wooden boutique style hangers for her clothes to replace the white plastic hangars she had. She needed about 220 hangers to get started since she had so much clothes. I placed an order on Walmart.com and the rest is history. Minami exclaimed, "Hell yeah!"

Twin Peaks had scheduled a Send Off Party Bikini night for Carrissa before her National Competition for a late June Thursday evening. I would not have the opportunity to attend since I am on the Board of Directors for the Santa Fe Area Home Builder's Association and we meet the third Thursday each month. I told everyone that I would try to go later in the evening upon my return to Albuquerque.

I was seated at the green L shaped sofa sectional in my mid century living room watching TV when Minami walked up from behind and asked, "Does this bikini top look neon to you?"

I was almost afraid to turn around as Minami handed me the bikini top. It was heavily padded. She was wearing a UNM T shirt with athletic shorts.

"Minami," I asked, "Where are your boobs?"

She laughed so hard, "I know, right?"

"You are the master of the push up padded bra. One could never tell. I noticed that night you came over in that gray dress." I said now also laughing. "Carrissa and most of the girls have implants, you know. Even Spicy Kim, that Vietnamese girl."

"I know, Bret,…" Minami continued, "I've considered having implants, maybe after I turn 21 in July. Not here either, I'm going to Scottsdale where the surgeons are better. All the girls who get boob jobs in Albuquerque get ugly scars and their boobs are so crooked. They only look good in a top. I want to look good naked when I get my boobs done."

"It would be tough to top a Range Rover, but with your birthday next month in July, I would consider boobs from Scottsdale for Minami!" I boasted.

"Really, Bret!Really? You would buy me some boobs? You're so cool,…why are you so cool Bret?" Minami was screaming.

"I said I would *consider* boobs from Scottsdale. Your Range Rover brakes need service the way they squeak and leave brake dust all over the rims." I replied.

"You are a man of your word,…" Minami giggled, "I am sure you will get me some new boobs." Yes again with the pearl white killer movie star smile and twinkle in her eyes.

Okay, so back to Thursday, Santa Fe Board of Directors, brakes for "her" Range Rover and the Bikini Night Send Off Party at Twin Peaks for Carrissa.

Minami and I dropped off "her" Range Rover for brakes full well knowing that the vehicle would be finished around 8 A.M. Friday morning. I encouraged Minami to take the yellow H 2 Hummer to Twin Peaks for her shift and she had concerns that everyone knows "it" is Bret's Hummer.

"So what." I said," No big deal,…I will try to stop in when I return from Santa Fe. Andrew and a bunch of people are coming for the Carrissa Bikini Send Off party."

I had a full day in Santa Fe on Thursday visiting clients and distributors. ABC Supply had their Founders Day BBQ and Food Drive. I had cleared out some canned goods from my kitchen and made a nice donation. The Board of Directors Meeting was canceled so that meant I would arrive in Albuquerque around 5 P.M. I was psyched.

I started to text Andrew about the possibility of needing a ride on Friday morning and he subsequently replied in text with, "Does this have anything to do with Minami's Range Rover?"

I sent a text back explaining it was no big deal if he could not help with a ride in the morning. I let Andrew know that I would arrive at Twin Peaks around 5 P.M. since my Santa Fe trip was cut short.

As I came off I 25 and down the frontage road in front of Twin Peaks I noticed the big yellow H 2 Hummer parked at P.F. Changs in clear view of the bar at Twin Peaks. The parking lot at Twin Peaks was like a circus full of cars, trucks, motorcycles,…I started to navigate the all black Chevy Tahoe into the parking lot when I received a call that "her" Range Rover was finished and I could pick it up at 8 A.M. tomorrow morning as planned or now before the shop closes at 6 P.M. I made a detour for "her" Range Rover. I could swap out the Hummer for "her" Range Rover later in the evening .

I went to Suncare and parked the all black Chevy Tahoe, walked to the nearby shop and grabbed "her" Range Rover, then drove to Suncare. I had a brief tan session and the girls at the counter asked how I was able to bring both "her" Range Rover and the all black Chevy Tahoe. "And where is your Hummer?" Then I gassed up "her" Range Rover and even a car wash. Minami is always out of gas in "her" Range Rover. I asked my neighbor Ms. Sanchez, a sweet Cuban lady with crazy Latin black curly hair, if she could drive me to Suncare for the all black Chevy Tahoe. When I bought my home way back in 2001, the Sanchez family already lived next door as they had when their home when built in 1991. They were cool neighbors and the owners of Roxy the dog. They always thought I was a bit goofy with women coming over and the big yellow H 2 Hummer and such. On the way Ms. Sanchez asked me about Minami and "her" Range Rover. Ms. Sanchez is only a year older than I and not one to judge after all the crazy years of being my neighbor I told her everything with just a few details omitted. The entire time my phone rang three times and three voice messages left. No number on the caller ID, only PRIVATE. I wondered if it could be someone from corporate in Anaheim since it was now 7 P.M. in New Mexico. I could not understand who would be calling me.

In the all black Chevy Tahoe I proceeded to Walmart to purchase several bottles of Gatorade to bring to New Mexico Plaster and Supply on Friday morning. It was there in the Walmart parking lot that I decided to listen to the voicemail on my phone....

Chapter Six

Actions Speak Louder Than Words /
Share a Stressful Scary Moment Together

Minami would get to see first hand my true colors...

Are you ready for this?

The voicemail on my phone went something like this... "This is officer Blah Blah from the Albuquerque police. You are the owner of a yellow H 2 Hummer which was apparently stolen and dumped near I 25 and Jefferson. We need You to come get your vehicle."

My initial thought was, *Yeah right,...how would the cops get my work phone number? It's just Andrew and the guys messing with me because they know Minami drove the Hummer to Twin Peaks for her shift. It did sound a lot like Jeff, Andrew's brother in law on the voicemail.* I went home and started laundry. Remember, I wash whites on Thursday night, towels, T shirts, and Ralph Lauren boxer briefs. As I was loading the machine I noticed the red blinking light on my old school 20th Century digital answering machine.

Yep,...same damn message about my yellow H 2 Hummer being stolen and I had the same feelings about being fucked with by Andrew and the guys. When I started to get that acid burning feel in my gut again, I stopped the laundry and drove to Twin Peaks in the all black Chevy Tahoe. It was now between 10:30 P.M. and 11 P.M. The yellow H 2 Hummer was clearly not parked at P.F. Changs or Twin Peaks. The lot at Peaks had several open spaces and I parked. I thought that maybe Minami had gone home already. I went in the side door from the patio and asked a bikini clad blonde "Is Minami working?"

"Yes Minami is working," the bikini clad blonde answered,"Would you like to sit in her section?"

"No." I responded staying calm and cool like George Clooney, "Please tell her that the police called and the car she drove to work today has been stolen."

Minami came walking up also in a bikini and still again with the killer movie star smile and twinkle in her eye. There are not enough words in a thesaurus to get a decent description of how hot she looked. Just take my word for it. I have a BA in Fine Arts from The Colorado College class of 1987 for Christ Sake.

"Where did you park the Hummer?" I asked Minami.

"Right over,..." she said as she pointed to the P.F. Changs lot sana big yellow H 2 Hummer. She became very stoic and serious. Clearly she felt awful.

I told her to relax and keep working her shift as I would call 242-COPS the famous Albuquerque Police non emergency line.

Just then as we stood outside in the Peaks lot the bikini clad blonde asked,"Minami, what happened, your car was stolen tonight?"

"NO…I drove his Hummer to work and it was stolen." Minami said as she pointed at me.

"Your Hummer was stolen?" asked the bikini clad blonde in disbelief,"I would be losing my shit right now. How can you stay so calm?"

Slowly, the remaining bikini clad Twin Peaks servers and bartenders came outside and moved their cars to spaces in the lot close to the front of the building. Despite the circumstances and not knowing where my Hummer was located and or the condition of my Hummer, the event was quite comical. The male operator at APD non emergency was polite and provided a case number as well as the location of my Hummer. Since I had not responded to four messages, the vehicle was listed as abandoned and a tow company had my beast. The operator provided the number of the tow yard. I asked about damage and he replied with the information that nothing appeared on the report except steering column,…No damage reported on the exterior.

I phoned the tow company and they confirmed the police information. Yes, they had my Hummer, steering column damage, NO exterior damage. It would cost $230 to recover my Hummer and I could not come tonight, only in the morning after 8 A.M.

Cool. I explained everything to Minami and she said that she would take an Uber home at the end of her shift.

"Fuck that!" I exclaimed. "Just text me and I will come back for you,…I'm doing laundry."

At 1 A.M. I went back to Peaks for Minami. She explained that since her contact lenses were bothering her and she had the appearance of crying, her manager did not make her close out the shift.

Her wooden boutique style clothes hangars,…all 220 of them had arrived and so her and I had a good laugh while we unpacked them from the Walmart.com boxes. Finally around 3 A.M. I jumped into bed so I could catch a couple hours of sleep before work and the subsequent reunion with the yellow H 2 Hummer at the tow yard.

Wes, our plant manager, provided me with a ride to the tow yard near Paseo del Norte on the extreme far north of Albuquerque. The office as sleek and modern with dry stack ledge stone on the walls and a shiny granite counter top. The man behind that shiny granite counter top informed me that he would need my license and registration. I tossed my license across the shiny granite counter, "I hope the registration is with the vehicle."

"Go ahead and walk back there, " Said the man behind the shiny granite counter.

Wes and I ventured over a sea of dry crunchy gravel past at least 100 severely damaged cars of all types in all types of crushed damaged, hopeless, ugly..

"Hey!" I yelled happy and excited, "there it is along the back wall." Yes, no mistake sitting all huge and proud was my yellow H 2 Hummer...

I entered in the passenger door so I could get at the registration in the glove box. Sections of the plastic steering column were on the passenger seat as were a few pieces of Minami's costume jewelry and gold chains.

"Hand me your key," Wes said as I tossed him the keys and he attempted to mess with the ignition. "I hate to force it in." Clearly, the key would not enter the ignition.

"Damn it !" I said frustrated, "Oh well, this is a tow company, maybe they can tow my ass to a Chevy dealer to get the ignition fixed."

Wes found my homemade anti-theft sign on the floor of the Hummer. I keep the sign on the sun visor and I believe that the sign saved the Hummer.

The sign has the Albuquerque Police logo and it reads in bold dark print:

SMILE FOR THE CAMERA!
YOU'RE IN A BAIT CAR
RELAX AND WAIT FOR THE HANDCUFFS

Albuqureque is one of the car theft capitals of the U.S.A. with an average 28 cars stolen daily,...Yes...daily...

As Wes and I started the walk back to the sleek modern office with dry stack ledge stone and shiny granite counter, it hit me. So help me as that sea of dry crunchy gravel under our feet made so much noise. I ran back to the Hummer and jumped inside and stuck the key in the ignition as far as it would go, turned the key,....and Vroom,... that famous General Motors engine purred as she started.

Since I needed cash for the $230 to release my "stolen" yellow H 2 Hummer, Wes drove me to a nearby Wells Fargo branch with an ATM. Upon our return to the tow yard, while I was inside the office paying the bill and obtaining a receipt, Wes reassembled and repaired all of the plastic sections from the steering column.

I had sent a trxt to my boss Joe earlier about the theft and impound. He replied with a text, "Go ahead- take as much time as you need."

Wes followed me home where I parked the yellow H 2 Hummer in the garage and went through the house and out the front door so Wes could drive us back to the plant. Minami did not even stir. I swear she is in a coma her sleep is so deep sometimes. The entire adventure was just barely over an hour. I had a productive Friday.

Once I called it a day and went home around 6 PM I was unable to start the Hummer due to a dead battery. With the aid of a 16 foot jumper cable and very close parking in the garage with the all black Chevy Tahoe, I was able to jump start the yellow H 2 Hummer. The instrument panel was not working and something was keeping the power on, draining the battery. I peeked at a couple YouTube videos and started to mess with all of the fuses.

Suddenly,...Minami pulled into the driveway in "her" Range Rover dressed in her vey sexy all black gym wear with crop top showing off her six pack abs.

"I called in since my contact lenses were still bothering me." She explained.

"Wow, " I replied,"*You* missing a Friday night, bikini night, gold mine, money maker at Twin Peaks?"

Minami had asked what I was doing and I lied and mentioned how I was just cleaning things up. I did not want her to feel any worse about the Hummer theft.

On Saturday morning Minami called in again to Peaks stating that she would not work the evening shift because her contact lenses were bugging her. When she finally got all dolled up in her sexy all black gym wear and drove off to her work out in "her" Range Rover,... I sprang into action. I messed with the Hummer, watched more YouTube videos, smacked the key with a hammer hard, forcing it into the ignition as seen on a YouTube video. I did all this until my yellow sumbitch was running normal; gas guage worked, speedometer, all was well.

I knew that Minami had been crying and yeah, maybe her contact lenses did bother her. She explained later that she was overwhelmed by how calm and cool I was after the Hummer theft. I told her that the voicemails left by the Albuquerque police said, "We would like you to get your vehicle." Hence, I knew that it could not be that bad. FYI, I had an old cloth lanyard with a plastic name badge from a presentation or home show with one of my business cards. *That* is how the Albuquerque police knew to call my work number. Never again will I assume that it is people messing with me. I will answer and respond to calls concerning car theft and individuals clearly making the identification that they are with the Albuquerque police.

Source of Positive, YSC *You're So Cool! Keep Her Comfortable, *Always* Keep Your Cool No Matter What, Actions Speak Louder Than Words.

I had notified Paul, my insurance agent, about the entire deal and he attempted to get back the $230 for me but my deductable was $500 so no dice. Later in the following week, people contacted my insurance, saying the Hummer struck their vehicles and caused damage. My insurance company sent a third party company to take about a zillion pictures from all points around the Hummer. The lady taking the digital pictures told me, "I'm really *not* supposed to comment, but, I've been doing this line of work for a few years now. I see nothing that says this Hummer hit anybody's car."

I picked up a really wicked flower arrangement with red roses and stuff at Albertson's on Coors and Montano for Minami after she had managed to stay with me in my home as my house guest for a full calendar month. I left the flowers on the kitchen counter where she mixes her almond milk and protein shakes and eats spinach, with Siracha and imitation crab when she gets home from a shift at Peaks or a gym work out.

Minami was in her sweet gray dress one night, stating that she had a brief house warming party to attend for some friends. I insisted that she *not* go empty handed and I gave her a bottle of wine to take as a gift. Later upon her return, Minami had a traffic citation from the Bernalillo County Sherrif. It was only a warning for not having her headlights on at dusk. I laughed, "Good thing Minami has her name on the insurance card. That deputy probably just wanted to stop you since you are a hot young woman dring a cool Range Rover…"

"Yeah," She laughed back, "And, and, Bret, I had to slip that bottle of wine from the front seat to the rear floor as the cop walked up to the car after he stopped me."

"Aw shet!" I laughed even harder – *yes*, I said "Aw Shet!" in a Canadian accent. Remember I graduated with a BA in Fine Arts from The Colorado College, a Division I NCAA Hockey School. I often say, "Aw Shet!" or the ever popular "Aw Fawk!"

YSC,…*You're So Cool!

To save face over the wine bottle, twenty year old house guest Minami racing around Albuquerque in "her" Range Rover and getting stopped by a Bernalillo County Sherrif Deputy,…I brought up her birthday coming up in later in July.

One of my favorite movies is "Bedazzled" and my favorite part in the movie is when Elizabeth Hurley leans close to Brendan Frasier's ear and wispers, "I'm the Devil." I would lean in super close to Minami and wisper into her ear, "Everyone wants to be Minami right now…" I had a woman wisper into my ear once, "All the guys here want to be *you* right now." It was a busy crowded Dallas night club and I felt like a celebrity movie star when she did that. So, yeah, every so often, I leaned into Minami's ear to wisper…

Chapter Seven

Always Turn Topics Back into Positive-

I added Minami onto my Wells Fargo Platinum Visa account and told her that's the card she could use to pay for her boobs in Scottsdale. She hugged me so hard and was so happy. I told her to keep the boob job under 10 grand and be sure to save some cash on the card for new bra shopping later after she got her new boobs. I explainded that the card would arrive in about a week, just before her birthday. Minami was excited and said that she had researched the surgeons in Scottsdale and that she had a former Twin Peaks friend living there who would allow her to stay. "She said that it will be a blast and that we can run around with no shirts at her apartment, Bret." Minami happily told me of her friend.

"Well," I seriously answered, "You and I can run around without our shirts in my home right now if you want."

That was the very cool thing about Minami and me. We could say anything and laugh…damn we used to laugh so damn much that my sides would hurt.

"Why are you so cool, Bret?" Minami asked.

I just shrugged my shoulders, "You are so cool, too."

"I will never forget you, Bret." Minami said again with that killer movie star smile and twinkle in her eye.

I pointed at her boobs and said, "Yeah, if you ever do forget me, after you get those babies done…just look at your new boobs and you will always remember Bret."

Minami laughed and said, "Seriously You are so motivational. Teaching me about weekly meal prep and getting me motiovated to get a trainer and work for the body sculpting competition."

"Please, give yourself some credit, too." I said.

"Really, Bret, " Minami said as she gave me a hug,…her head resting on my chest since I am clearly an entire foot or more taller.

Then it hit me like a ton of bricks and I could not hold back. The build up from Minami was far too great,…I told her, "I love to spoil you so much so that it will ruin it for *all* the other guys in your life in the future."

Minami laughed.

Minami came home early from Twin Peaks one night, and while still in her uniform, with a grey hoodie over her torso, she and I had dinner standing in the kitchen at the counter. She was having her standard imitation crab and chopped spinach with Siracha sauce consumed with chopsticks, washed down with a thick parfait style protein shake made with almond milk…and…mixed with a chop stick and…eaten with a chop stick. Hey, it was thick chocolate parfait style protein shake with almond milk.

Minami looked at me with a sexy smile and batted her lashes,…"Hey, Bret, have you been taking notes?"

"Notes? Notes on what?" I asked.

"Notes on all of our experiences and adventures since we met in February." Minami answered as she took a bite of imitation crab and spinach with Siracha sauce plucked with her chopstick like the Asian pro chopsticker user that she had become.

"Wow, that was bar none the most sexy thing a woman has ever said to me…" I grinned.

How to Make a Woman Happy

She just shrugged her shoulders, smiled and winked at me, "You know how to make a woman happy."

Mmmm, she is such a pretty woman, this Minami, now my house guest, Twin Peaks Girl, and UNM Pre-Law student driving around in my pimp Range Rover. Oops, I mean driving around in "her" Range Rover...

Damn, I loved having dinner with her in my kitchen. Watching her eat with chopsticks and having profound conversations... .Mmmm...I am at a loss for words.

Once while she was driving "her" Range Rover and I in the passenger seat I noticed a small scar on her right arm above the elbow.

"When are you going to tell me abouth the South Valley Knife Fight?" I asked as I traced around the scar on her arm with my finger.

"It is not from a knife fight in the South Valley," Minami replied with a smile. She continued, "That is where one of my ex boyfriends shot me."

WTF.

"I thought he had taken my phone so I went to his house. And as I walked up the front sidewalk, he opened fire and I hit the ground." Minami explained still with her killer movie star smile and twinkle in her eye.

"Damn..." I said really slowly and ghetto, "Did anyone call the cops?"

"Yes," she continued more," The neighbors called because my ex had hit their house during the shooting. They (cops) handcuffed me with all kinds of blood running down my arm."

"What?!" I yelled.

"Well... *you* must have been causing the trouble," Minami said in a low police voice."He is well within his rights to shoot you advancing on his property."

Wow. .See? Often times we can make serious points with women just because the clods before us are so screwed up.

Her twenty-first birthday was soon approaching in late July.

I always wake super stupid early around 5 A.M. even on Saturday and Sunday mornings when I am off. Many times I will wake up around 3 A.M. when Minami comes in on Saturday and Sunday morning when she works a closing shift at Twin Peaks. I will hang with her in the kitchen while she eats her spinach and imitation crab with chopsticks,....sometimes some almond non dairy yogurt. We just laugh and laugh about... nothing... and anything.

Minami had arrived home around 3 A.M. after a closing shift and since I did not wake and join her in the kitchen, she slammed things around and made way too much noise. I sneaked in behind her and kissed the back of her neck, "Hey, if you want some company, just nudge my shoulder and wake me in bed..."

Mianami merely giggled and winked at me.

One particular Saturday morning after waking early, visiting with my parents on the phone about 6 A.M. as I do each and every Saturday morning, I wandered into the kitchen to grab something to eat. I was being extra special quiet so as not to disturb the sleeping beauty princess Minami. I buy those pre boiled and peeled eggs from the deli at Walmart and I pre cook a package of ten sausage links to keep ready. I cut the boiled egg in half and dribble some Valentina Mexican hot sauce. Usually followed by a small silver can of V8 Fruit Fusion Peach Mango juice. Mmmm, I drink (Slam!) a can of that juice first thing every morning. At any rate, when I finished with my breakfast and went to toss my paper towel in the trash, I noticed a butter knife in the trash can. WTF. Upon closer inspection I noticed it was a butter knife from Twin Peaks. Hmmm, Minami...

Later in the day,...like maybe around 12 noon when she woke all groggy but with her movie star smile and twinkle in her eyes anyway, Minami entered the kitchen to start her feeding routine with chopsticks.

"What the hell is this Twin Peaks butter knife doing in my trash?" I asked Minami as I tried to stay serious and not laugh.

She just smiled more and laughed, "Well,...it fell into my pouch and I guess I brought it home. I like to eat celery sticks with that jar of almond butter that I take to work anytime I get a chance to take a break."

"So, ..." I started, "You just cannot return the knife back to Peaks?"

Minami laughed as she hugged me tight.

"I may need to speak with your manager." I said as she squeezed my ribs and took my breath away. For being my favorite little Asian, she could really squeeze like a James Bond villan. She made me laugh with that last squeeze of my ribs.

One full calendar week prior to Minami's twenty=first birthday, I would have People's Flowers send one of the famous luxury rose arrangements with red roses and a few extra white roses too to Twin Peaks for Minami. She would bring this giant Hollywood movie star bundle of roses home and it took up the entire mid century modern conference table that I use for a dining room table.

I gave Minami a $200 plastic credit card type gift certificate to Nini's Nails and I also provided that particular gift before her birthday. Minami has the most amazing hands and feet. She splurges on the mani and pedi and it shows... Mmmm...Mmmm.

I had two gifts wrapped in birthday wrap with really cool gold ribbons. No, damnit, I am not gay. Minami likes gold things... and I have a BA in Fine Arts from The Colorado College. I freaking love birthdays and Christmas so I can wrap presents. I do a job like those sexy ladies at the Clinique counter in Macy's. I highly recommend you get some expensive ass perfume for a girlfriend some time and have it wrapped by those Macy's women. You get what you pay for.

Anyway, back to Minami's gifts. One big tall gift leaning on the wall and a small square box. I told her that my mom used to tease us about a week before our birthdays. Minami said, "Can I open one early since I will be spending my birthday with my mom and dad?"

"Mmmm... maybe at the stroke of midnight this Wednesday since your birthday is on Thursday." I answered.

Chapter Eight

Be a Man of Your Word, Attention Cycles-Push and Pull, Make Her Laugh, and Keep Her Comfortable

During one of our late night / early morning conversations in the kitchen just wearing T shirts and shorts, eating dairy free almond yogurt having a philosophical conversation, Minami said, "I knew the day we crashed the Peaks Bikini Car Wash with your big yellow Hummer, *you* were a man of your word, Bret."

"Stop!" I laughed, "You are making my head swell and I am getting conceited. How did You figure *Bret* was a man of his word?"

"When you placed that Range Rover key chain in my hands, I knew that you would really get a Range Rover for real." Minami said in a near wisper in the dim kitchen light.

"Seriously?" I inquired.

"Oh yes!" Minami answered with a devilish grin. She was also eating a thick chocolate protein shake made parfait style and eating the thick mud with a chopstick licking with her tongue. Oh so damn sexy.

"Well, …" I cut in ,"Just so you know, you did say that the Range Rover was your dream car…"

"Um hmm,"Minami hugged me.

"If you had said that a Nissan Juke was your dream car…" I hugged her back and continued with my dialogue, "It is doubtful I would have returned any of your calls or text messages…" I started to laugh as Minami pushed me away with her hands and began to devour her thick chocolate mess again with her chopstick.

"I need chores, Bret." Minami smiled at me and batted her lashes.

"Chores?" I asked, "What the hell do you mean, chores?" Like laundry… my laundry?"

"Yes," Minami answered back with another sweet grin and still batting her lashes. "When I lived with my parents they gave me chores…"

"Whoa !" I cut her off in mid sentence and in a calm cool George Clooney voice I leaned right next to her ear and said, "I'm *not* your parent,…"

"I know…" Minami started.

"You are my house guest…" I cut her off again before she could finish her sentence. "You may certainly do my laundry. Mmmm, …a big fantasy of mine to have a Twin Peaks girl move in and do my laundry."

Let's get one thing clear right now. I pretty much do her laundry or at least finish the laundry that she starts on a consistent and constant basis. No big deal, I enjoy folding her tiny clothes after the dryer cycle.

Late Sunday morning Minami bugged me about opening one of her birthday gifts, even though her birthday was not until Thursday.

"Well…?" Minami asked, "You know my mom has the evening planned and I will be with my family."

"Yeah, okay," I said sternly. "Maybe the big present."

"Yay! Thanks, Bret!" Minami screamed, "I think it's a big mirror…"

She looked so cute with *no* make up, bed hair, and wearing a grey UNM T shirt with black gym shorts. Mmmm… her body is so cut from daily gym training for that body sculpting competition and her special diet of imitation crab, chopped spinach, Siracha sauce, and thick chocolate parfait style protein shake with almond milk. She tore off the gift wrap and gold ribbon as if she were rescuing children from a burning building.

"OMG!" Minami shrieked. "I love the gold frame."

"It's a luxury mirror meant to lean on the wall." I said as I started to help her with the cardboard and Styrofoam pads. I lifted the entire mirror onto the twin bed as she was standing on the bed tearing away at the wraping and such.

While she stood on the bed looking so very sexy in her natural state with *no* make up, bed hair, grey UNM T shirt and black gym shorts I decided to grab her and give her a massive hug. Since she was standing on the bed, she was as tall as I.

She hugged me back and she squeezed my ribs so hard I felt a little fart 'pop' out through my ass cheeks. In all the excitement and ruffled gift wrap (it took an entire roll of new birthday gift wrap from Target to cover that giant luxury mirror) she did not hear my fart. Thank God!

"If I were getting new Boobs in Scottsdale, I would want a big ass luxury mirror with a gold frame to admire them,…" I said with an evil cackle.

Minami buried her head in my chest and hugged me again.

"Like I told you before, "I said, "I plan to spoil you and ruin it for all the guys in your future."

"Is *this* what it is supposed to be like?" Minami asked. "Is this what you do for women?"

Minami began to look at the remaining small square gift.

"Oh hell," I said, "Bring it to the kitchen and unwrap it at the table." Her big ass luxury rose arrangement from People's Flowers was still in bloom and thriving in the middle of my mid century modern conference table that I used for a dining table . "Now there are a couple presents in that box." I informed Minami.

She tore away at the gift wrap and gold ribbon asking if I had an Xacto knife. I provided Minami with the orange handle scissors from the untility drawer next to the stove in the kitchen.

First she took out the birthday card which said-

WISH BIG. WIN BIG. On the outside.

On the inside her card said-

Minami,

I've got a feeling some of your wildest dreams are coming true this year!

I signed the card with-

Very Happy 21st Birthday

*YSC

Bret XoXo

I then also taped on the card a fortune cookie from Panda Express which said:

ALL FRIENDS BEGIN AS STRANGERS

Her first little gift in the box was a stainless steel necklace of a fortune cookie with a tiny fortune that read:

EVERYTHING HAPPENS FOR A REASON

"Aw,." Minami said, "I'm going to hang this from the mirror of 'my' Range Rover."

The next gift was a black Nike tennis dress... very sexy and so damn cool... so I thought. I will not get into the details but Minami explained why her body would not look good in the Nike tennis dress.

The next gift was three tiny Calvin Klein thong panties, one black, one grey, and one white.

"I have done laundry on several occasions since you moved in, " I started, "And, I see no clear indication that Minami ever wears panties."

Minami began to laugh so hard, "Well, no I seldom wear panties, but,..." She would go on and on about sanitary conditions, hygene, etc., etc,.etc,....

"Well," I said with confidence, "If you choose not to wear the white thong panty, I want to use it for a pocket square with my black suit."

Minami laughed again and again.

Minami would later go to the gym for her daily training session and I would go to Suncare. That Sunday morning was one of the most fun times. We both laughed so hard our sides hurt.

On the Thursday night of her actual birthday, she arrived back here at my home around 9:30 P.M. and we visited for an hour or two,…Minami was a self proclaimed "introvert" and she was so smart, so sensitive, always in a great mood with that killer movie star smile and twinkle in her eye. She had arranged for an initial consultation meeting with a surgeon in Scottsdale on Friday, the third of August, next week.

Wow… before I get to where I drive Minami to the Albuquerque International Airport for her one day flight to Scottsadale and back in the same day for the breast augmentation procedure consultation, we should recap How To Make a Woman Happy…

Chapter Nine

Recap of How to Make a Woman Happy

No particular order with the exception of the First Impression- This is key, so be honest, interesting / Impress Her.

- Have great personal hygene-
- Dress well, use small amount of cologne, brush your teeth at least twice each day, shower, shave... all the stuff your *mom* was on you constantly about.

Have Confidence-

- No matter what, be strong and have confidence.
- Make Her Laugh and Be Charming-
- Stay positive and use light humor.

Attention Cycles-

- Do not smother her, be around, and give her space.
- Text on the phone-
- Great communication, do not over do it. Skip a day, answer her, but use balance.

Eye Contact-

- Eye contact is a must when you are in person.

Use Her Name-

- Use her name and use her name often.
- Favor Effect (aka Ben Franklin Effect)
- Ask her to do a favor- she will like you.
- Go Big or Go Home… Big Favors… trust me…
- Build Trust and Rapport-

Offer a key to your place, loan your car,…yeah,…even if you own the original model year yellow H 2 Hummer just like the Hummer featured in the hit HBO series Entourage.

- Smile Often-
- Smile Often and Be Positive- She will return the smiles.
- Flirt and Tease-
- Be nice and use with caution to be endearing and not hurtful.
- Empathy-
- Know her and feel her experiences. Listen to her…
- Listen-
- Listen to her and pay attention.
- Do Not Pressure Her-
- Be a man of your word and come through for her.
- Make Her Comfortable-
- Actions speak louder than words.

How to Make a Woman Happy

I understand that not every man tears around in a yellow H 2 Hummer and that not every man lives alone in a James Bond – Dean Martin cool mid century modern pad with stacked ledge stone all the way up to the vaulted ceiling and a Zen garden in the backyard. Work on it. Evan was one of my bartenders at Bennigan's and when he was just getting started in real estate he sold me a 1200 square foot home. Over the years I fixed the place up into what it is today. The house payment is less than most apartment rent for a month. I have all kinds of cool dishes, bar ware, wine goblets, Champagne flutes, margarita glasses, cocktail shakers, chop sticks,…props like the men in the movies. I have cloth napkins and long stick candles, too.

Eat beans and do what you must to have money. Pinch pennies and get the best job you can find and do not settle or stop looking until you find the best job with great pay and hours. If you want to spoil a woman, you will need money.

Now "her" Range Rover is not the first time I have purchased a car for a woman. I once bought a big ass very cool 1983 K5 Full Size Chevy Blazer with custom mag wheels for the mother of my kids. In 1998 I bought my girlfriend, Jhovana, an all black Dodge Avenger, when the Avenger was the cool manual transmission two door sports coupe. Mmmm, sweet vehicle. I bought Banda, my favorite Mexican, a Nissan Murano, also all black, because she said that was her dream car.

I have four credit union accounts, a Wells Fargo Savings, as well as a Bank of America Savings with Mutual Funds, and a crazy 401k from my job. Learn to save and build credit.

Years ago I knew a woman who was a personal trainer and also worked at Hooters, Tiffany Rock Star. We were good friends. Such good friends in fact that she called me on a Sunday, just as I was about to watch a Bronco game on TV and she asked if I had laundry, cooking, or cleaning for her to do since her hours had been cut. She came to my house and raked some leaves in the yard. I topped the tank in her Mustang and gave her $40 cash. I later got her a case of Snapple. I bought some wings, quesadillas, onion rings, and assorted items to go for one of my million dollar distributors and she clocked out and drove with me to serve the food at my million dollar distributor,…in her Hooters uniform. The guys working at that distributor were so impressed about a Hooters girl coming with Bret to deliver lunch right on their front counter. Those guys still talk about that stunt several years later.

Treat a woman so special that she will remember *you* forever. Behave as if that woman will be on a TV talk show like Jimmy Kimmel or Connan O'Brian and you obviously will want her to say some damn nice things about how *cool* you were with her back in the day.

In an interview I watched on TV once with Angie Dickinson, the actress had been a co-star in a western with John Wayne, when she was really young. She went on and on how John Wayne wore such nice cologne and he was such a gentleman. He was not a grab ass flirt. I am paraphrasing but Angie said of John Wayne, "He was such a great guy."

Life is short and we should never play games. Treat them so well and special that it will ruin it for the guys who follow after you. Should things not work out, just be a gentleman and move on. No need to have hard feelings.

Just be genuine and interesting. Stand out from the guys. Be a man like the men in the movies. Be original.

*Extra… Why I drive that 2003 yellow H 2 Hummer?

Ever since the hit TV series Entourage was on HBO I had to own a yellow H 2 Hummer. I was not sure how I could ever afford the beast,…Deal with the Devil? Law of Attraction? I hunted and hunted for just the right deal. In the summer of 2007 I found my particular model at Cross Country Auto near the Cottonwood Mall in Albuquerque for about $40 grand. I asked Rajah, our sexy receptionist, to call and tell them that I was in El Paso searching for a Hummer at Bravo Motors. Get details on the Hummer from Cross Country and then ask if the price was negotiable. Later in the week I returned right after lunch with Evan, my original real estate agent whom I purchased my home and I worked with at Bennigan's in 1998. I was the senior manager and he was a bartender. Evan is a Jew who prides himself when it concerns negotiation and intimidation of the sale of anything. I took a test drive and after informed the salesman that the price was way too high for a pre-owened Hummer and I would be better off purchasing a *new* Chevy Tahoe. The salesman reminded me that 2003 was the original actual model year for Hummer and this vehicle would sell fast. Ugh. I returned to work and after a series of phone calls from the salesman, the price dropped to $30K and I returned around 5:30 P.M. that day, with Evan and $3,500 cash for a down payment. There was *no* down payment required and when the salesman asked if I was happy financing the Hummer at $30K I asked, "If I pay cash can we go even lower?" He did not call my bluff and I did not possess the capacity or cash anyway. Due to a need for floor mats and extra remote key, I refused possession of the Hummer until the salesman delivered to my corporate office late in the afternoon on the following day, with my requested floor mats and extra remote key. Oh, and the yellow Hummer was on fumes. Why do freaking car dealers do that? We had a real cool corporate office before moving down to the current office at the plant in 2010. That same summer I had the CD for Fergie's solo album and I used to jam on the stereo her song, "Glamorous" so damn loud in my yellow H 2 Hummer.

Chapter Ten

Be a Man Like the Men in the Movies

This is a true story of how I met Minami, three days after Valentine's Day in February and by the first week in August, she was living with me, driving "her" Range Rover, on my car insurance and on her way to get a breast enhancement.

I understand that my examples are extreme, but use the examples in different scale and perspective. You cannot live with your mom or your grandma unless you are very unselfishly helping them due to poor health. Roommates...? Bah,... never!

Indiana Jones, James Bond,... George Clooney, Brad Pitt,... Dean Martin,... live alone in cool pads. Er,... or with sexy girlfriends.

YSC. *You're So Cool

Okay, okay,... let's get back to Minami and her trip to Scottsdale....

We hardly slept the Thursday night before, both way too excited. She spent the usual routine of getting ready, hair, make up, spinach, imitation crab, Siracha sauce, thick chocolate parfait style protein shake with almond milk, all consumed with chop sticks. She looked so hot in all black, tight athletic shorts, and a long sleeve all black top with her Nike shoes... she looked like a celebrity.

As I mentioned before, I took her to the airport in the all black Chevy Tahoe and as I pulled up the the curb at the Southwest Airlines Terminal, I jumped out and ran around the front of the vehicle so I could give Minami a big hug before her trip. I gave her a big kiss on her forehead and said, "Text me when you get there, have a good trip,…see you tonight!"

All the people in the immediate area looked dumbfounded since she had no luggage and I suspect due to what I just said. Her return flight was at 9:30 that same night.

I could hardly work all day. My office at the plant is right near the Albuquerque International Airport. Actually, we are located just on the other side of Intersate 25 and the end of the runway brings the flight path directly over our plant. Kirtland U.S. Air Force Base is also located next to the Albuquerque International Airport and when those fighter jets take off, one would swear they will strike the silo where we manufacture stucco. Anytime a FedEx plane comes in for a landing I always yell,"Hey, here comes my Victoria's Secret order… " It used to be damn funny, but now Wes, the plant manager, and his crew just roll their eyes at me.

As it was getting near the time to venture back to the airport for Minami for her 9:30 P.M. arrival, she sent a text that her flight was delayed and she would not arrive until 1:30 A.M. Saturday. She added that she would just take Uber home.

I sent a text back and let her know, "No way on Uber," and I would be there.

I was watching old Seinfeld re-runs on TV about ready to make the drive to the airport when it hit me. Albuquerque became big in the motion picture industry with many major motion pictures and TV shows like Breaking Bad, In Plain Sight, Better Call Saul. Once on a flight from John Wayne Airport in Orange County, we hung out with Paul Ben Victor, the famous character actor. He was on the TV series In Plain Sight and catching Southwest Airlines back to Albuquerque. We gave him drink coupons and he had a glass of wine. I asked if I could give him a ride in my yellow H 2 Hummer and he said that the studio would provide transportation.

I sent Minami a text that I would meet her at the bottom of the escalator near baggage claim. She had no bags since she was only on a one day trip. No matter. The city managed parking garage right across from the terminals only charges about three bucks if one parks a car there for less than an hour. Sometimes the ladies at the gate do not charge me at all. I hope I do not get anyone in trouble with that remark. I love to get people from the Albuquerque International Airport.

I put on an all black suit with an all black tie and crisp white dress shirt. No pocket square. Limo driver appearance. I wrote in a big fat Sharpie pen in black ink on a big business size 10" x 14" envelope YSC. Remember YSC means, "You're So Cool" and Minami and I text that shit over and over all the time.

As people wandered around the terminal looking at me I could tell they wondered who I was there to collect. It seemed like an eternity, but soon, I noticed those famous Minami legs appear coming down the escalator, then a puzzled look, then she recognized me, then that big glow of a movie star smile and her twinkle in her tired eyes from a very long day.

"You're crazy," she said sleepily.

"Just walk normal and follow me," I said as I tossed my YSC sign in a trash can. "All these people are trying to figure out who you are..."

It was so exciting. I had the all black Chevy Tahoe in the first space next to the stairs in the parking garage. A quik zip through the gates, $3 bucks later with a little friendly banter with the lady working the toll booth at the gate, and we were on Interstate 25 headed for the Big I, west on Interstate 40, off on Coors, and briefly to my pad in Taylor Ranch. It is so easy and convenient to zip around Albuquerque… especially after 1:30 A.M.

"Tell me all about the *best* part of your Scottsdale visit." I told Minami.

"Well…" she started, "I go back this Wednesday, procedure scheduled on Thursday afternoon at 3 P.M., silicone implants and I return on Saturday evening!" Minami was so excited she could hardly contain herself.

"Outstanding, my favorite little Asian…!" I exclaimed, "I am so damn happy for you."

"I cannot tell you how much you motivate me, Bret." Minami continued. "I probably would have not done my boobs until I was in my 30s…"

"Whatever, Minami…" I laughed. "Yep, you love me now but after in pain, you will say, 'Damn you, Bret, damn you!'"

From Saturday until Wednesday we could hardly contain the excitement. She would say things like, "Why are you so cool?"

After some time I would ask, "Hey Minami,… I have a question."

"Yes?" she would respond.

"Why are *you* so cool?" I would laugh.

Minami would come back with, "Why are *you* so cool?"

"Hey I asked *you* first. Why are *you* so Cool?" I would ask again, laughing.

"Don't you just hate when people aswer questions with a question?" Minami would chuckle.

She was getting ready for the gym in her sexy all black movie star Kardashian style workout gear complete with black Nike sports shoes. She had her cool jug of water as she said, "Bret,… I feel like a bum."

"Hey!" I yelled as I jumped in front of her coming out of the kitchen with my arms at my sides like a riot police officer. "Bums do not drive Range Rovers, and bums do not get boobs in Scottsdale."

Minami hugged me with one of those deep squeeze around my ribs again with her head resting on my chest right under my chin.

"Damn you, Minami!" I laughed and laughed. Oh shit, Minami can make me laugh by doing nothing but hugging me and squeezing my ribs.

Monday at lunch I and Cisco from work went to Panda Express. Cisco had asked if Minami had all of her stuff moved into my home by now.

"She still has a few things in her POD at the storage facility like that big California king bed." I answered.

"Tell her that storage is a waste of money and get the rest of her things to your home." Cisco said.

"Yeah right. " I smarted off, "She has so much shit in my house now it would take an entire big ass green Mayflower tractor trailor rig to move her out and at least a week to do it."

"Have them drop that POD in your driveway." Cisco was certain he knew how to help,…even if no help was required.

That evening Minami asked, "Hey Bretm can I have that POD delivered over here and placed in your driveway?" Damn crazy coincidence!

"Sure, sweetie." I bravely answered, "I can park the all black Chevy Tahoe on the street. Just ask that they face the door towards the garage and place the POD a few feet away from the garage so I can get the Hummer out."

WTF what was I thinking? Still *no* POD in my drive way yet as I write this draft.

That week Minami worked Monday and Tuesday nights at Peaks and came home early each night around 9:30. She had actually given notice with her manager about leaving without a clear or defined final last day of work. Perhaps that Tuesday would be her last day at Twin Peaks. Minami told her parents about the Scottsdale appointment and she spent a few hours with her mom on Tuesday night. After her return to my home, we hardly slept on Tuesday and the running around getting ready ritual Wednesday morning went so fast. She packed light with logic how Wednesday was travel, Thursday the procedure, Friday recovery, and Saturday the return flight.

I told Minami, "The manager at Peaks probably will not allow you to quit. Instead they will want you to train the other girls. Think about it… you served Bret just one time and now you are driving a super cool late model Range Rover, you are on Bret's car insurance, you live with Bret for free room and board, Bret ends up doing your laundry a lot of the time,…and you will soon have a set of free boobs from Scottsdale."

Minami only laughed with *no* comment.

"It seems like just yesterday I was asking you, 'Minami, where are your boobs?'" I would ask and laugh.

"I know, right?" Minami said with her killer movie star smile and twinkle in her eye.

"After you get them done,…" I started waving my finger and pointing at her boobs, "Can we call them Brets instead of Breasts? You know, Bret augmentation?"

Minami laughed so crazy hard, "Well, I guess,…*you* are paying for them."

We were laughing and carrying on so bad we both had tears in our eyes.

"I know a few girls who disputed the charge on their Visa after and they got their boobs for free." Minami said.

"Naw, " I laughed more, "That is bad karma."

Once again at the Southwest Airlines Terminal in the all black Chevy Tahoe I got out and ran around the front to hug Minami and grab her carry-on bag from the back seat.

Chapter Eleven

It Is a Positive Thing When You Miss Each Other- Time Apart

I did not hear from Minami all day Thursday. I sent a few short unanswered text messages,... four to be exact. *Maybe she is sleeping?* I thought. That woman can sleep all day. On Friday I sent two text messages to *no* reply. Since Minami is so strong I did not worry. However, I did have a peculiar sensation that something was not right. I did not have the number of the friend where she was staying. On Saturday I figured I would just play it cool and go get her from the airport that evening.

At about 3:20 in the afternoon I got a text from Minami that said, "I'm back home with my mom. I'm in a insane amount of pain." She had her friend drive her six hours from Scottsdale on Saturday morning. We bantered with just a few short text messages. I told with a text for her to be strong and manage the pain. "Tell your body that this was your choice, pain is understood but no longer welcome."

We had more brief text messages on Sunday and Monday. I told Minami that everything happens for a reason and sometimes with more than one reason. I added that this was quality time now with her and her mom. I also joked that this was the Universe reminding her about the contemplation to dispute the Visa charge and get free boobs. Bad karma.

Minami sent the standard "LOL" text.

On Monday, I shipped across town a small box of her favorite Nature Valley Biscuits with Almond Butter and my copy of the book by Jen Sincero, YOU are a BADASS, since Minami had mentioned time and time again how she wanted to read it. The lady at the UPS store thought I was a doofus paying $9 bucks to ship a small box to just the other side of Albuquerque. I explained that it was for a sick friend. Then I remembered a YouTube video I watched about the Alpha Male and how the Alpha Male needs not explain things....

Tuesday was the scheduled window tint appointment for "her" Range Rover. I went to the place on Lomas and waited while they did their magic. I sent a text to Andrew about meeting for lunch and we decided Papadeaux's around 12:30 and Andrew mentioned he would bring a friend, Daniel, one of the owners from Quanz Auto.

I had to stop near Winrock Center Mall and snap a quik pic of "her" Range Rover with the new dark window tint and text to Minami. She really liked the pic and said her pain was still there,... not quite as bad as Saturday and her mom was taking super good care of her.

After lunch at Pappadeaux's, Andrew and his friend Daniel and I visited in the parking lot for a few minutes. Andrew had arrived in his Ferrari and his friend Daniel Quanz was driving a bright chile pepper red Tesla. Mr. Quanz, standing next to the sleek vehicle and using his smart phone, started the motor of the Tesla, ...and, ...wait for it, ... using his smart phone, backed the Tesla from it's parking space.

Here I was so proud of the window tint on "her" Range Rover. It must have been during all this activity that I missed the text from Minami, "I will be at the house in about 30 minutes." I replied that I would meet her there and I raced home. How cool,... it had been six straight days that we had not been in contact.

She was wearing her black work out shorts with a gold Puma logo and a short sleeve olive drab button down shirt that I had never noticed before. Virtually *all* of her clothes and things were in my home.

"Hey,..." I gently said to her. "You look great,...really. I was concerned you would go too big."

Minami smiled but it was obvious she still had some discomfort, "Well, I am swollen and everything will drop down and get to a better size."

I helped her make a chocolate protein shake with almond milk mixing with a chopstick and thick parfait style the way Minami likes it.

She also ate some imitation crab and spinach, telling me that she had to be careful since she had been having trouble keeping food down since returning home on Saturday. Minami had a Walgreens prescription for muscle relaxers and Ibuprophen.

"The Uber driver lady was so sweet, " Minami told me,"She said it was okay for me to run in Walgreens and get my prescriptions. Did *you* miss me, Bret?"

"Hell yes! Of course I missed *you*... Can I drive you home?" I asked

She violently shook her head no and I did not push it. We have a significant age difference if you have been paying attention. No need to shock her parents.

"I plan to come back and stay with you on Wednesday but more likely on Thursday." She said.

"Cool, " I answered with, "The rims and tires arrived today and Discount is open until 6 P.M.,...They said I can come in today for install on *your* Range Rover."

"I can't wait to see everything when it is finished." Minami yelped with a smile.

Minami had arranged for another Uber to take her back to her parents home. We sat and drank some Dasani bottled water (I keep it by the case in my giant M TV Crib's monster fridge). I encouraged her to wait before taking the muscle relaxer or Ibuprophen until she was at her parent's house. Minami said that she still needed help in the shower and she asked if I could replace the shower head in the bathroom and get one with the hand held unit so she could spray her body.

"Of course I can," was all I needed to tell Minami, my favorite little Asian. She knew that Bret is a man of his word and that she is spoiled. Hence, yes, the new dual shower head with hand held spray was installed that same evening.

It was sad to watch her go. I placed her things in a Walmart grey plastic bag so she could carry them more easily. She was still so sore from the new Scottsdale boobs and she had limited upper movement with her arms. Oh yeah, Minami smiled,…not quite the Hollywood movie star smile, but there was still a smile. The twinkle in her eyes was covered by a pair of aviator sunglasses. I am certain that twinkle in her eyes was still there. Wow,…All I could think of was, *Hey Minami,…where are your boobs?* And *Bret, you are so motivational to me…*"

Not in any way attempting to turn things and make this about me,…However, I felt like such a shit. Minami was in a lot of physical pain and emotional slump since she was staying with her parents, not working, and not going to the gym everyday.

I took "her" Range Rover to Discount for the custom rims that had arrived from California and the Yokahama tires.

When Discount finished and asked me to wait by the front door outside, "her" Range Rover looked so damn incredible as the Discount employee drove up. I was compelled to snap a pic and text to Minami. She was floored and excited.

I had previously ordered a key fob from Range Rover of Albuquerque and they were ready to program the device on Thursday. I scheduled as early as possible at 8 A.M. so I could still get up before 5 A.M. and have a productive morning before and after my time having

How to Make a Woman Happy

"her" Range Rover serviced. The Range Rover- Jaguar Dealer was cool the way I like with a mid century modern vibe, stacked ledge stone and all. I sat in an over-sized comfy brown leather chair. A slender attractive young woman dropped by to inform me that they had snacks and coffee. I proudly told her, "Thanks." She smiled. I wandered around and was looking at the most recent Range Rover models in the showroom when a salesman asked if he could help. I told him that I had my 2013 Range Rover Sport in the service bay having a new key fob programmed. He asked how I liked my Range Rover and other sales banter,…yadda, yadda,…let me know if I can help,…

When "her" Range Rover was finished the tech mentioned how very super clean and obviously well cared for the vehicle appeared.

"Thanks,…" I said meekly, "It is actually my wife's Range Rover, I seldom drive it." Wow…Did I really say that? I guess I did. I was not ashamed of "her" Range Rover. It just came out. I wanted to take another pic after I paid for the service as "her" Range Rover was parked under a celebrity movie star canopy. It did not seem appropriate, so I did not snap a pic. They had mentioned that "her" Range Rover was in excellent shape and that they had re-programmed the electric system and the check engine light was now off. They even programmed the garage door opener located in the rear view mirror. Wow,…what service.

I had sent a text for my good friend Peggy to meet me for lunch on the patio at Bravo! Italian in the Uptown Center. I raced home with "her" Range Rover and swapped out with the all black Chevy Tahoe.

Thursday came and went,…No Minami. I sent a text of a picture which displayed the instrument panel from "her" Range Rover and it said, "Look- No More Check Engine Light."

When I returned from a long ass Friday at work, "her" Range Rover was not in the garage. I was so excited. I ran into the house.

There was a set of chopsticks in the dishwasher and a paper plate in the trash. She had eaten. She had brought quite a few new items into the bathroom and there were a few things in her walk in closet that used to be a spare room. Her Peaks uniform and booties were still there as were her gym work out clothes and water bottle. She spent the night with her parents and returned Saturday morning.

"I have a surprise for you, Bret," she told me excited, "Give me five minutes."

It was a small bundle of sage in a seashell. Minami burns sage often around bed time,…amazing stuff.

"Last May when I stayed here and you were in Dallas,…" Minami began to say, "I was so comfortable on the lawn out back in your Zen garden."

"Yes I know,…*You* told me already." I informed her.

"Yeah, but I never told you how I was so relaxed that I fell asleep on the lawn." Minami said still with her Hollywood movie star smile and twinkle in her eye. "I woke and moved to the couch in the living room and slept more."

"Well,…so *you* sleep a lot,…"I said, "No secret, Minami sleeps all day,…"

"No,…" Minami interrupted my sarcasm, "I was so relaxed here,…I knew that I would stay with you soon. I just knew that I would move in to this house,…It is so *fun* to be here. I am so happy. You're my best friend right now, Bret. Don't make jokes and tease all the time."

Long story short, Minami started her senior year at UNM this week. She is back to living with me after a few days recovering from her boob augmentation (Bret Augmentation) staying with her mom, and she made a comment about how "cool" the new shower head and hand held shower are that I installed. She asked me if I could get a dingy dress of hers white again and when I did, she mentioned ,

How to Make a Woman Happy

"You're So Cool, Bret!" It will take around six weks total for her Bret Augmentation to stop hurting, heal, and look supreme. I think her boobs look great now.

Minami loves "her" Range Rover, especially with the new tinted windows, special black custom rims from California, and Yokahama tires. She asked if I could get the Wall Street Journal delivered here at the house as she needs it for one of her classes.

Naturally I now have a subscription with the Wall Street Journal delivered to my home.

I pride myself in understanding how to keep a woman happy.

YSC,...*You're So Cool !